Exploring Place Value

Ann Butler, Mo Cregan, Lucy Duncan, Sheila Ebbutt,
Denise Handley, Trisha Henley, Hazel House, Maureen Klingels,
Jon Kurta, Frances Lindemann, Karren Mortimore, Fran Mosley,
Jean Roberts, Lorenzo Salzano, Melanie Widnall and Jenny Youdell

Project Director	Sheila Ebbutt
Project Editor	Fran Mosley
BEAM Project devised by	Lynda Maple and Anita Straker

We are very grateful to the many people who have contributed to this book, by suggesting ideas, or by trialling activities in schools. In particular we would like to thank:

In Islington
Mel Ahmet and Thornhill Primary School
Shirley Beswick and Canonbury Infants' School
Naomi Brest and William Tyndale Primary School
Catherine Clark and Prior Weston Primary School
Kim Connor and St John Evangelist Primary School
Sarah Duckham and St Mary's CE Primary School
Sophie Norburn, Sarah Tilling and Penton Primary School
John Spooner and Rotherfield Junior School

Elsewhere
Peter Clarke and St Margaret Clitherow RC Primary School, Brent
Lorenzo Salzano and Meadows Primary School, Nottingham
Jean Millar, the teachers of Ashmole School, and the Lambeth BEAM group
Andrew Warren and St Mary and St Michael RC Primary School, Guernsey
Val Jerram, Carden County Junior School, and the Brighton BEAM group
Maureen Johnson and Bellfield Middle School, High Wycombe
Christine Pugh and Hazelbury Infants School, Edmonton
Joe Buchan and Kilham CE Primary School, Humberside
Kath Kelly and All Souls RC Primary School, Salford
Helen Williams, Education Consultant, Cornwall

Copyright © 1995 BEAM, Barnsbury Complex, Offord Road, London N1 1QH
All rights reserved. The whole of this book remains subject to copyright, but permission is granted to copy the photocopiable sheets for use only in the school which has purchased the book.

ISBN 1 874099 26 X
Designed and typeset by Bookcraft, Stroud
Illustrations on children's game-sheets by Butterfly Design, Bowker Vale
Cover designed by Charles and Juliet Snape Ltd, London
Printed by GPS Ltd, Watford

CONTENTS

Introduction	4
What is in this book	4
Place value in the curriculum	4
Using the activities	5
Assessment and record-keeping	6
Layout of the activity pages	8
Learning about place value	10
The Activities	11
Photocopiables	47
Resources	63

Activities	*levels* 1	2	3	4	5	6	*page*
Vegeburgers	★	.	.	.	.	.	12
Cubist	★	★	.	.	.	.	14
Collections	★	★	.	.	.	.	16
Pass the Papers	★	★	★	★	★	.	18
Tens or Ones?	.	★	.	.	.	.	20
Swaps	.	★	★	.	.	.	22
Jigsaws	.	★	★	.	.	.	24
Count	.	★	★	.	.	.	26
Add 5	.	★	★	.	.	.	28
Where Is It?	.	★	★	.	.	.	30
Times Ten	.	★	★	★	.	.	32
Skittles	.	★	★	★	.	.	34
How Many Dots?	.	.	★	★	★	.	36
Quadraville	.	.	★	★	★	.	38
How Big is a Million?	.	.	★	★	★	.	40
Target 500	.	.	★	★	★	★	42
How Long is a Million?	.	.	.	★	★	★	44

INTRODUCTION

What is in this book

The activities
There are 17 core activities in this book, and they are designed for you, the teacher, to read — you can then decide how to present each one to children. Each activity takes up two pages and, with its extensions, can provide a substantial amount of work for individuals or groups of children. The first page describes the activity, its extensions and what questions to ask children to promote their thinking; the second provides information on using the activity — the mathematics involved, what to look for in assessing children's understanding, and much more. Detailed information about how the activity pages are laid out is offered on pages 8 and 9.

The photocopiable sheets
Several of the activities require children to use photocopied sheets — some describe games, others offer some form of worksheet. All these are provided towards the back of the book in the form of pages which can be photocopied and given to children.

Place value checklist
It is not always easy to find one's way through a particular area of the curriculum, and to recognise which aspects of learning it is most important to offer children. To make this easier for you, on page 10 we have provided a list of:
— the important experiences which children need to have
— the facts which children need to know
— the important ideas they need to develop about place value with whole numbers.

Place value in the curriculum

Work on place value needs to start early in a child's school life. At this stage a child may know little about numbers over 10, but they can get used to ideas such as completing a set and exchanging — the kinds of idea developed in the activities Vegeburgers and Cubist. You can help children meet these ideas in all sorts of ways, through work on money, counters, base ten blocks (and blocks in other bases) and so on.

Having started work on the earlier concepts, children should return to work on place value at regular intervals in primary school, in order to develop their understanding further. Understanding place value is very important if they are to feel confident about the structure of our number system by the time they reach secondary school.

The activities in this book mostly concern whole numbers, but older children working on place value will begin to explore decimal numbers, and see how numbers smaller than one follow the same rules as other numbers. The BEAM activity book *Exploring Decimals* contains activities on decimals for older children — see *Resources* on page 65.

The recording done by two six-year-olds of their work on the activity 'Times Ten'

Using the activities

Choosing an introductory activity

The first time that you do one of the activities in this book with children, it is a good idea to choose one that is appropriate for a wide range of levels. You can treat this as an introductory activity, both for the children and yourself. You could work with the whole class (many of the activities are sufficiently open for children to work at different levels on the same one), or with a group.

If possible, observe each of the children and notice how they are reacting to the activity. It is also important to discuss the activity with the children. Encourage them to explain and share their ideas and hunches, and also to talk about their feelings — their excitements, frustrations and so on.

Moving on

Once you have begun to get a picture of how individual children have reacted to the work, you should look through the rest of the activities. This will help you get an overview of the range available, and so assign activities to children at an appropriate level. You may find, at a later date, that you need to readjust your judgements about children — they have 'off days' and 'on days', and it is very easy when doing assessments to put children at a higher, or lower, level than is comfortable for them.

When you have decided about the level appropriate to each child, you can organise work on the next activities so that groups of children who are roughly at the same level work together. Of course you can experiment with different ways of organising the children, and there may well be occasions when you want mixed-ability groupings. But on the whole same-level groupings are best as they enable children to be more truly collaborative in their work together.

When choosing activities it is important to remember that children working on the same activity may well tackle it at different levels, according to their different degrees of sophistication and confidence. It may sometimes be worthwhile encouraging a child to try and work at a higher level than she or he appears to be doing, but at other times you may well feel that children have decided for themselves the level appropriate to them.

Amy		Octaville
1		2-0
2	1-1	2-1
	1-2	
3	1-3	2-2
4	1-4	2-3
		2-4
5	1-5	2-5
6	1-6	2-6
		2-7
7	1-7	2-8
10		2-9

One child, Amy, really enjoyed working on the activity 'Octaville' and found it quite easy — until she got into the higher numbers, when she began to make mistakes. She was able to offer her teacher a clear explanation of what she did.

Assessment and record-keeping

Using the sampling sheet in this book

Many systems of record-keeping will tell you *what* a child has done, but often there is little room for comments on *how* she or he has done. The photocopiable sampling sheet which you will find towards the end of this book has been designed to help you keep a record of how a child is working in various strands of development, including both the what and the how.

It is not possible to make detailed assessments of every activity, but you could use an activity from this book or another source as a focus for sampling children's work on, say, a termly basis. (The sampling sheet is divided into three sections for just this purpose.) The headings under which you make your observations are fairly self-explanatory, but on the next page we offer some questions to bear in mind when filling in the sheet.

How and when to assess

Obviously how and when you make these detailed assessments will depend partly on the organisation of your classroom. However, there are certain guidelines which teachers have found useful when trialling these materials. It seems to work best if you organise the class so that you can sit with a group of children, as an observer rather than as an active teacher. You will need to watch and listen, and also to talk with each child about what they are doing, bearing in mind that your role here is to learn about the child rather than to teach.

The process of observational assessment becomes quicker the more you do it. As you and your colleagues gain evidence about children's learning in mathematics you will be able to discuss how to use that knowledge to benefit continuity and progression throughout the school.

Keeping a cumulative record

You could keep one piece of a child's work, as well as the sampling sheet, in a folder bearing that child's name. You can write the date on each piece of work, and any extra comments about what you observed while the child was working on it and what emerged in discussion with the child. Over time, this sample and other significant pieces of work will provide a useful record of the child's progress, for use in the school, for discussion with parents and with the child, and at transfer to a new school.

Children's self-assessment

Towards the end of this book you will also find a photocopiable children's record sheet. These sheets can be used to encourage children to reflect on the work they have done, and consider what they have learnt from it. The sheets are particularly useful in providing a record of practical activity. They can be put in the child's work folder or stuck in a child's book as a reminder that mathematical work did take place — even though there was 'nothing to show' for it.

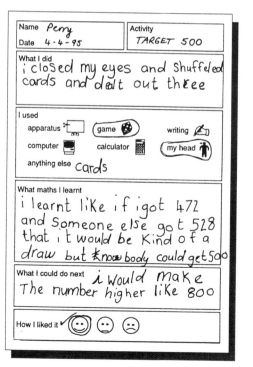

One boy's record of a completed activity

Name of activity and source
What activity was the child doing, and where did it come from?

Social context and personal qualities
It is a good idea to assess a range of contexts over the year so that you have the opportunity to look at how the child operates in different social groupings. Was the child working on their own, with a companion, in a small group, alone with an adult, in a group with an adult? Did the child show evidence of any of the following qualities: confidence, initiative and creativity, persistence, cooperative effort, interest, enjoyment?

Mathematical Content
What mathematics has the child shown they understand, and at what levels? (You can be flexible here, writing down part of one or more level descriptions.) Although work on place value is most likely to relate to the programme of study in number, we have included other areas, as the child may touch on work in these areas.

Using and Applying Mathematics

Problem solving
Did the child decide what mathematics and what materials to use to work on the problem?
How did they organise and work through the problem?
What outcomes did they reach?
Did they check their work? If so, how?

Developing mathematical language
What language did the child use to discuss the work?
How did the child record the work?
How did they present their work to others?

Developing mathematical reasoning
What hypothesising or generalising did the child do?
What evidence did you see of the child's reasoning and use of logic?

LAYOUT OF THE ACTIVITY PAGES

Ask the children to...
These are instructions for you, the teacher, to convey to the children in your own way. When these activities were being trialled, most teachers felt that it was not helpful for the card to suggest the exact words.

Useful questions
In the bubbles below the main activity there are questions you might ask children. These can help them take a step forward in their thinking as well as providing you with a quick assessment of their understanding.

What if...
These are ideas for extending the activity by changing one aspect of it, or by pursuing related investigations. Often it is when working on the extensions to an activity that children develop the broader understanding that is so important to their understanding of mathematics.

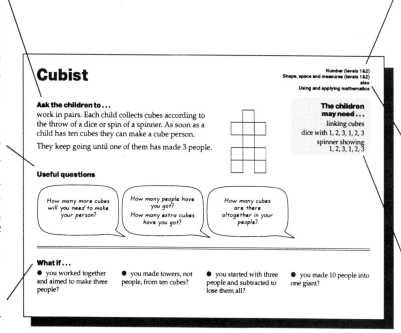

Programmes of study
Each card shows the main areas of the curriculum which the activity covers. All exploratory mathematics will also involve 'using and applying mathematics', so this is nearly always shown. You may find that some children, especially if they decide to extend the work their own way, also explore areas not mentioned here.

Levels
Different children doing an activity from the same card may engage with the problem at various levels, so we have suggested a range of levels rather than just one.

The children may need...
This is a list of materials that need to be available to the children doing an activity. With some activities the materials are essential; with others the presence in the classroom of suitable materials can give children the opportunity to select what to use for themselves.

Aims

A brief outline of the aims of the activity.

Assessment points

Questions to ask yourself about what the child has demonstrated in doing the activity. The answers to these questions will tell you whether the child has grasped the important ideas behind the activity.

Mathematical background information

Under this heading comes any important information which you may need about the mathematics involved in the activity.

Organisation

In trialling these activities teachers sometimes pointed out organisational details which may make a difference to how well the activity works. Where appropriate, they are mentioned here.

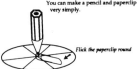

Bubbles

These refer to the 'useful questions' bubbles and offer reasons why you might pose the questions.

What if ...

Further suggestions about how or why to extend the activity.

Possible contexts

This section suggests topics, projects or other classroom work with which this mathematical activity might fit.

LEARNING ABOUT PLACE VALUE

What follows is a list of what children need to experience and understand about place value with whole numbers (decimals are not included here). Although some of the ideas are in rough order of complexity, there is no clear progression — children will not all follow the same route through these ideas.

Children need experience of:

counting
- counting objects below 10
- counting objects to 10, then 100, then 1000 and beyond
- reading and saying numbers to 10, then 100, then 1000 and beyond
- writing numbers to 10, then 100, then 1000 and beyond
- putting in order numbers to 10, then 100, then 1000 and beyond
- exploring numbers as big as a million and above
- reading a calculator display
- exchanging a set of objects for a single object of equal value (for example, with base ten blocks, replacing ten 'ones' with a ten-piece)

grouping and exchange
- grouping objects to show the number of subgroups and ones left over (for example, showing 9 as four groups of 2 with 1 left over)
- grouping objects in tens and ones as a means of counting the whole set
- looking at objects grouped in tens and ones and saying the number of objects in the whole set
- grouping objects in hundreds, tens and ones as a means of counting the whole set
- looking at objects grouped in hundreds, tens and ones and saying the number of objects in the whole set
- activities involving exchange and decomposition (for example, exchanging five 1p pieces for one 5p piece and vice versa)

manipulating numbers
- counting on and back in ones, twos, threes, fours, fives from 0 and from any number
- counting on and back in tens, twenties and hundreds from 0 and from any number
- partitioning numbers in different ways (for example, 76 as 60 + 16 and as 70 + 6)
- doing calculations using their own methods, including mental ones
- doing calculations using place value
- multiplying and dividing numbers by 10 and 100
- working with a range of apparatus (calculator, number line, structured apparatus, pencil and paper, everyday objects)
- rounding numbers up or down to the nearest ten, hundred or thousand

Children need to know and understand:
- the idea of a group or set
- what each numeral in a multi-digit number represents (for example, in the number 345, the '3' represents three hundreds, the '4' four tens and the '5' five units)
- that our base ten system is only one of many possible systems
- that elsewhere in the world, and at other times in history, other number systems have been used
- when and how to use rounding up or down and approximation
- the effect of multiplying and dividing numbers by 10 and 100

THE ACTIVITIES

Vegeburgers

Number (level 1)
also
Using and applying mathematics

Ask the children to...

get into pairs and play the *Vegeburger* game — in the *Photocopiables* section following page 48.

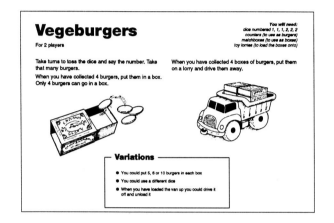

The children may need...

Vegeburgers game-sheet
dice with 1, 1, 1, 2, 2, 2
'burgers' (counters)
'boxes' (match boxes)
'lorries' (toy lorries)

Useful questions

> What does the dice say?
> How many burgers must you take?

> How many burgers have you now?
> How many more do you need before you get a box?

> How many boxes and burgers have you got?
> What do you still need in order to fill the lorry?

What if...

- you put 6, or even 10, burgers in each box instead of 4 — and 6 (or 10) boxes in a van?

- you used a different dice?

- you filled up the van first and then made a game of unloading it?

- instead of burgers you collected pennies to exchange for 10p pieces and then finally swapped those for a £1 coin.

- you collected base ten blocks, and aimed for 100 — or started with 100 and tried to reduce it to 0?

Aims

- grouping in tens
- experiencing the idea of equivalence
- experience of exchanging
- experience of decomposition

Assessment points

Can children:
— count to 4 accurately?
— say how many more burgers they need to fill a box?
— say how many more boxes and burgers they need to fill a lorry?

Organisation

Children can play this game either competitively or collaboratively.

Instead of providing toy lorries you could give the children cut-outs, or get them to draw their own. (Drawing them big enough to fit four matchboxes is a good exercise in measures.)

This game can go quite quickly. It is a good idea to have an idea of what you intend the children to do next — perhaps record their work, play with a different dice, teach this game to a friend, or invent their own version.

Bubble 1

It is a good idea to get children to say their dice numbers out loud — it encourages their partners to monitor what they do, and discourages cheating.

Bubble 2

Encourage children to think ahead, and work out how many burgers they need to get to fill a box.

Bubble 3

This question can be quite challenging, as children need to look at both how many burgers and how many boxes they have.

What if ...

Unloading the lorry would involve starting with a lorry loaded with four boxes, each containing four burgers, and aiming to reach 0.

Some children will benefit from playing the money version, collecting pennies to exchange for a 10p piece, and then eventually exchanging ten 10p pieces for a pound coin.

You can make similar games to suit any class topic: children round a table and tables in a room (for a project on 'School'), peaches in a box and boxes on a lorry (for 'Other Countries') and so on.

Possible contexts

This activity can be adapted to the collecting of other things instead of vegeburgers, depending on what topics the class is currently working on.

Cubist

Number (levels 1&2)
Shape, space and measures (levels 1&2)
also
Using and applying mathematics

Ask the children to...

work in pairs. Each child collects cubes according to the throw of a dice or spin of a spinner. As soon as a child has ten cubes they can make a cube person.

They keep going until one of them has made 3 people.

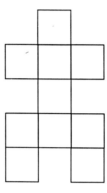

The children may need...
linking cubes
dice with 1, 2, 3, 1, 2, 3
spinner showing 1, 2, 3, 1, 2, 3

Useful questions

How many more cubes will you need to make your person?

How many people have you got?
How many extra cubes have you got?

How many cubes are there altogether in your people?

What if...

- you worked together and aimed to make three people?
- you made towers, not people, from ten cubes?
- you started with three people and subtracted to lose them all?
- you made 10 people into one giant?

14

Aims

- counting
- practical experience of addition
- grouping in tens

Assessment points

Can children:
— count to ten accurately?
— say what they have collected so far (for example 'one person and 3 cubes')
— say how many more cubes they need to make ten?

Mathematical background information

Counting up to 10 and then regrouping is a key concept in place value. This game will encourage children to think of 10 as an important number, the point at which they regroup.

Organisation

Have plenty of cubes ready. With some children you will want to provide base boards showing the outline of a person; other children may be able to follow a prototype produced by you; others will be able to make and agree a model person with ten cubes to copy during the game; others may not want to follow a pattern but prefer to invent their own.

You can make a pencil and paperclip spinner very simply.

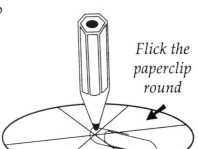

Flick the paperclip round

Bubble 1

This question, 'How many more do you need?' requires children to count things that are not yet there. This can make it a difficult question to answer, but one that children need to learn to handle.

Bubble 2

One way of focusing children on grouping is to encourage them to describe their results so far — for example, 'One person and three cubes', 'Two people and seven cubes'.

Bubble 3

This gives you an opportunity to find out how the children count. Do they need to count all the cubes from the start, or do they count in tens, then add on the ones?

What if ...

Children sometimes find that making their cubes into a person is hard, and get distracted from the basic activity. If this happens you could suggest everyone makes a tower with their cubes. This allows children to compare their towers and check that they are all the same height.

Possible contexts

This activity can be adapted to the making of other models, depending on the topics the class is currently working on.

Collections

Number (levels 1&2)
also
Using and applying mathematics

Ask the children to...

work in a group of three or four. Children take turns to toss a dice, and take the corresponding number of 'ones'. At the end of each turn, if they have a set of ten ones, they exchange it for a 10-piece.

They continue like this until the players have all collected five 10-pieces.

Useful questions

- *How many ones is that collection worth?*
- *How many more 10-pieces do you need to reach 50?*
- *Do you need to get exactly 50, or can you go over? Does it matter if we disagree about this?*

The children may need...
base ten blocks
linking cubes in sticks of ten
straws and rubber bands
dice
coins
place value mats

What if...

- you aimed for 100 instead of 50?
- you aimed for 500, using tens and units dice?
- you used two dice instead of one?
- you collected 1p, 10p and £1 coins instead of tens and ones?
- you started with a 100-block and took pieces away until you reach 0?
- you started with a £1 coin and took pennies away until you reach 0?

Aims

- understanding that ten ones are equivalent to 1 ten
- experience of exchanging and decomposition
- 'reading' how many there are in a collection by looking at the sets of tens and ones

Assessment points

Can children:
— see when they need to exchange ten ones for a 10-piece?
— say how many ones a collection is worth?
— put out number tablets or cards to match a collection of tens and ones?

Mathematical background information

Some children need a lot of experience with this kind of activity before they fully understand that the 'name' for a number of objects simply describes how many tens and ones there are in the set.

Organisation

Children who find this idea difficult need to explore many variations of the activity. One possibility is to time the game, and stop it after, say, 3 minutes. The children then put out number cards to show how many tens and how many ones they have, and 'read' you the number. The person with the highest number is the winner.

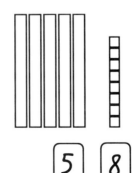

Bubble 1

You may want to help children count the tens and ones and then say the number with them — for example, 'Six tens and eight ones. That's sixty and eight. Sixty-eight'.

Bubble 2

Encourage children to think, not just about how many they have, but how many more they need.

Bubble 3

This is an opportunity for children to decide on their own rules. What rules they agree on does not matter too much. What is important is for them to understand the idea that rules can be made up — they are not just 'there'.

What if ...

All kinds of extension activity are possible. Children who are used to handling money may find coins helpful. For a simple exchange activity use 1p, 10p and 50p coins (paralleling the activity as it works with base ten blocks). You could extend the activity to include a wider range of coins, including 2p, 5p, 20p and £1 pieces — children can choose what and when to exchange, and what total sum to aim for.

Children could use two dice and simply add the two numbers and collect that many 'ones', or one dice could be a 'tens-dice' and the other a 'ones-dice'.

You could use blocks in bases other than ten. This would reinforce the idea of exchanging and help children see that ten is just one of many possible bases for a number system.

Pass the Papers

Number (levels 1-5)
also
Using and applying mathematics

Ask the children to...

sit in a circle. One child shuffles the cards and deals one to each person. Now everyone needs a piece of paper. They write their number at the top left and, when everyone is done, pass it to the person on their left. Everyone writes the next number in the series, and passes it on again, and so on. As soon as someone writes down 100 the game is over.

The children may need...
pencils and paper
number cards 0-50
number line

Useful questions

> What is the number that has just been written on your paper? And the next number you need to write?

> How do you write the number after 39? How do you write the number after 40?

> Is anyone writing a number close to 100? How far from 100 is your number?

What if...

- we started with numbers over 50 and went back towards 0?
- we started with numbers over 100 and went forward to 200?
- we added 2, 5 or 10 each time?
- we used decimal or fractional numbers?
- we started with a negative number?

18

Aims

- experience of writing numbers up to 100 in order
- practice dealing with zero as a place holder

Assessment points

Can children:
- write each of the digits 0-9 the right way round?
- write two-digit numbers with the digits in the right order?
- write the next number after a 'nine-number' such as 59?
- write the numbers up to 100 in the correct order?

Organisation

It is a good idea to have a number line available for children to refer to if they are not sure how to handle the change from, for example, 29 to 30, or 79 to 80. With young children you might want to sit around a table so that everyone can see clearly whom to pass their papers on to.

You could introduce this activity to a large group. Once children are familiar with the structure of the game, they can get into smaller groups and play it at their own level (see suggestions in *What if . . .*).

You will need to experiment to find your preferred way of writing the numbers — some teachers like to get children writing their numbers in columns, one below another.

```
78    84
79    85
80    86
81
82
83
```

Bubble 1

You can help children by encouraging them to find their numbers on the number line and by saying the numbers with them — 'That number is a 3 and a 4. That's right: it's 34'.

Bubble 2

Again, referring to the number line can help children who are not sure how to write the numbers.

Bubble 1

This question reminds children of the aim of the activity. They can get so involved in the task of writing numbers that they forget they are working towards 100.

What if . . .

This activity is very versatile and can be adapted for children at all levels of attainment. Children can add 2, 5, 7, or 20 each time . . .

They can work with decimal or vulgar fractions . . .

They can start with a number under 10 and double each time . . .

Or they can work with numbers below 0.

```
0.1  0.2  0.3
0.4  0.5  0.6
0.7  0.8  0.9
1.0  1.1
```

Tens or Ones?

Number (level 2)
also
Using and applying mathematics

Ask the children to...

work together to 'walk' along a number line from 0 to 100. They do this by tossing both dice, and using a felt-tipped pen to draw their steps.

  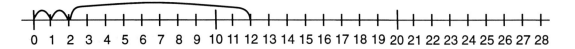

Useful questions

Don't forget — you only count steps forward. Don't count the marker you are on.

Can you move forwards 10 without counting each step? How can you do that?

You are on 67 and you've thrown 'two tens'. Where will that take you to?

The children may need...

number line 0-100

felt-tipped pens

a dice showing *tens, tens, tens, ones, ones, ones*

a dice numbered 1, 1, 1, 2, 2, 2

What if...

- you showed the number line you've just used to a friend and challenged them to tell you what the dice said each time?

- you used a line numbered –50 to +50?

- you made a record of your moves?

- you used three dice — the two you already have and one showing *backwards* on two faces and *forwards* on four faces?

- you walked back from 100 towards 0?

- you made this into a game?

Aims

- exploring the difference between a '1' which stands for 'one' and a '1' which stands for 'ten'
- exploring the effect of adding ten and its multiples to any number
- becoming familiar with the number line

Assessment points

Can children:

— make and count single steps accurately, backwards and forwards?

— make and count jumps of 10 accurately, backwards and forwards?

— predict where they will end up after they have made a set of steps (up to 9)?

— predict where they will land when they have made one or two ten-jumps?

Organisation

Children will need to use the kind of number line that can be drawn on and wiped clean (see *Resources* on page 63).

An alternative to using a number line is to use strips of squared paper, 101 squares long, numbered 0-100. Children could make steps with a finger and colour in where they land each time.

Some children may enjoy playing this competitively, two of them racing along the line to reach the end before the other.

Bubble 1

It is important that children learn that a step should take them forwards and they should not count the marker they are on.

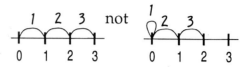

Bubble 2

This question links with one of the *What if . . .* suggestions. Looking back over the steps and jumps they or other children have drawn will also highlight any errors, such as drawing a ten-jump that takes them from 19 to 28.

Bubble 3

Encourage children to predict where they will end up before they draw their steps or jumps.

What if . . .

If children make a record of the stopping places on their journey along the line, they can see clearly the effect of moving on in tens.

```
 3
 5
15
16
26
46
```

Children can use the same dice to collect base ten blocks until they reach 100, or display beads on an abacus. Both of these can provide useful reinforcement of the mathematics behind the activity, and show different ways of looking at place value.

An alternative activity uses an unnumbered line with 100 intervals. Children take cards one by one from a pack of 0-100 cards and find where to write the number by making ten-jumps and single steps.

Swaps

Number (levels 2&3)
also
Using and applying mathematics

Ask the children to...

play *Swaps* with a friend — the game-sheet for *Swaps* is in the *Photocopiables* section following page 47.

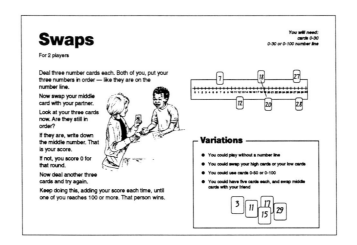

The children may need...

Swaps game-sheet
cards 0-30
cards 0-100
two 0-30 number lines
0-100 number lines
number tablets
numbered counters
playing cards
calculators
dice

Useful questions

- Are you sure your cards are in the right order? How do you know?
- After you swap, are your three cards still in order? Why is that?
- How can you keep a record of your score?

What if...

- you had five cards instead of three?
- you generated your three numbers using dice instead of cards?

- you used cards up to 100 and aimed for a higher total score?

- you used number cards from −50 to +50 and a number line going from −50 to +50?

- you used number cards showing decimal numbers between 0 and 10 such as 3.5, 5.4 and 1.3? What sort of number line would it be best to use?

Aims

- practising putting numbers in order to 50 or 100
- becoming familiar with the number line model of number
- practising addition skills, with a calculator or mentally
- thinking about probabilities

Assessment points

Can children:
— put three cards (0-30) in order accurately?
— put three cards (0-100) in order accurately?

Mathematical background information

Children will need to understand that they have to pay attention to the tens digit before the units digit when putting numbers in order.

Organisation

Children could make their own number line and number cards or tablets. A number line showing numbers 0-20 or 0-30 could be made big enough to hold the number cards or tablets.

It helps if you have different coloured cards for each player. The children could keep their cards when they win — this helps with keeping track of the score.

Once children understand what is meant by 'putting the numbers in order' they may well be able to discard the number line.

Bubble 1

This question provides a useful assessment of children's understanding.

Bubble 2

Children may expect the middle cards always to fit when they swap them over. They will need to compare their high and low numbers with their partner, perhaps ringing them on a number line, and discuss how the numbers fit in relation to each other.

Bubble 3

Children could use calculators to keep score.

What if ...

With five cards the swap is less likely to 'work', so the game will last longer.

If children aim for targets over 100, they may need to use calculators to keep track of their scores.

This game can be adapted and used as a way of familiarising children with negative numbers — as long as children have met such numbers and have a rough understanding of what they are. Children can use a number line with 100 intervals, numbered in ones from −50 to +50, and corresponding number cards.

Children can also play this game with decimal numbers. We suggest a number line with 100 intervals, numbered in tenths from 0 to 10, and corresponding number cards.

Jigsaws

Number (levels 2&3)
also
Using and applying mathematics

Ask the children to...

do the 100-square jigsaw using the international script — this is in the *Photocopiables* section. Then ask them to do the one in Bengali script.

The children may need...
jigsaw pieces (international script)
jigsaw pieces (Bengali script)
squared paper

Useful questions

> Can you find the piece with number one on?
> Read me the sequence of numbers from one.

> Can you read out that row of numbers?
> What number do you need next?

> What patterns can you see so far?
> Are there any other patterns?

What if...

- you made up a number script of your own?
- you investigated other number scripts used in the world?

- you made a 100-square (or 25-square or other number grid) and used it to make a jigsaw of your own?

- you wrote numbers 1 to 100 in a spiral and made a jigsaw from them?

- you made a jigsaw showing numbers –50 to +50?

Aims
- thinking about what each digit in a two-digit number represents
- thinking about how the international number system works
- thinking about how other number systems work
- exploring number patterns

Assessment points
Can children:
— say the name of any number (in the international script)?
— describe number patterns they notice in either script?
— look at any number and say what number comes next?

Mathematical background information
The Bengali script follows the same system as the one used internationally, but uses different symbols. Working with this script, whether children are familiar with it or not, will help them see the parallels with the international script and so get a deeper sense of the structure that is common to both systems.

0	1	2	3	4	5	6	7	8	9
০	১	২	৩	৪	৫	৬	৭	৮	৯
10	11	12	13	14	15	6	17	18	19
১০	১১	১২	১৩	১৪	১৫	১৬	১৭	১৮	১৯

Organisation
There are two sheets in the *Photocopiables* section of the book, showing a 100-square in the international number script, and the same square in Bengali. Both squares have thick lines which you should cut along to make jigsaw pieces for this activity.

Unless children are familiar with Bengali numbers, they should do the international numbers jigsaw first. They will use or develop strategies which they can then put to use in doing the Bengali jigsaw.

Bubble 1
If children are stuck get them to look for the pieces with single-digit numbers on first.

Bubble 2
Children will use various strategies. A useful strategy for those who need help is to read a sequence of numbers until it runs out, then look for the piece with the next number on.

Bubble 3
Looking at the pattern of the numbers can help children see what number they need next.

What if...
This activity can be adapted in many ways. Less confident children can make their own jigsaws from ready-made 100-squares, later moving on to preparing their own number squares (either to 100 or a lower number) and turning them into jigsaws for each other.

Other children will readily take to making their own variations of the 100-square — with numbers going up and down, or round in a spiral, or in an oblong rather than a square grid.

Count

Number (levels 2&3)
also
Using and applying mathematics

Ask the children to...

estimate how many beans there are in the jar and mark their estimates on a number line. Now ask the children to tip out the beans and count them. The correct answer should also be marked on the number line.

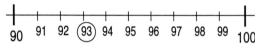

Useful questions

> How are you counting the beans?
> Can you make sure you don't lose count?

> How many beans have you got?
> Can you check?

> Was your estimate close to the real number?
> How close?

The children may need...

number line 0-100
number line 0-500
jam jar filled with beans/paper clips/ conkers/pennies/ pegs/cotton reels
number tablets or cards (0-9)
miniature honey jar

What if...

- you filled the same jar with smaller/larger objects?
- you used a mixture of objects?

- you collected different jars and filled each one with the same kind of object?

- you collected lots of the same kind of jar and filled each one with different objects?

- you fitted as many tiny things as possible in a miniature jar?

Aims

- grouping sets of objects in tens and ones
- knowing how to 'read' a number of objects grouped in tens and ones
- finding and reading numbers on a number line

Assessment points

Can children:

— count a smallish number of objects by grouping in twos or fives?

— count a larger number of objects by grouping in tens?

— find any number up to 30/50/100 on the number line?

— use single-digit number cards to represent the number of tens and of ones in a set and 'read' the total number of objects from the cards?

Organisation

You can 'fix' this activity by careful choice of jars and objects, so that less confident children are working with smaller numbers of objects (say, under 30, 50 or 100), and more confident children are working with larger numbers (say, 100 to 500).

This is an excellent assessment activity, which can help you judge how firmly a child grasps the basic principles of place value. Some children, while able to count in twos up to 30, will not be able to group in tens. They will need more work at this level.

A child who confidently counts in tens — and regroups into hundreds where appropriate — is ready to move on to work with larger numbers and with decimals.

Bubble 1

Children who understand the principle of grouping in tens may still need help with practical aspects such as keeping the sets tidy and organised.

Bubble 2

A well-organised count can be interrupted and restarted, or checked, at any time.

Bubble 3

Try to help children see that comparing the count with the estimate is not a question of right and wrong, but rather that estimates can be improved with practice.

What if . . .

A class could spend a week investigating 'How many things fit in a . . .'. Children can each work at their own level, while listening to, and learning from others working at different levels.

Children enjoy finding as many different things as they can to fit in small containers such as miniature honey jars or matchboxes. However an alternative is to use their small container and fill it with a quantity of same objects and see how many can be got to fit. They can then try with other objects. Will the jar hold more paper clips then safety pins? More sunflower seeds than rice grains?

Add 5

**Number (levels 2&3)
also
Using and applying mathematics**

Ask the children to...

take turns to pick a number card at random and put that number in the display of a calculator. Ask them to add 5 to that number. If both digits in the display change they keep the card. If only one digit changes they put the card to the bottom of the pack.

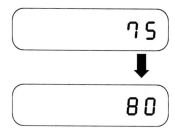

The children may need...
number line 0-100
felt-tipped pens
calculators
number cards 10-90

Useful questions

- What numbers are on the cards you kept? And on the cards you put back?
- Can you predict whether you will get to keep that card? Why will you/won't you?
- Are you getting to keep more cards than you put back? Why is that?

What if...

- you chose which card to take each time?
- you added 1, 2, 4 or 9 instead of 5?
- you recorded the additions on a number line?
- you used an abacus to add 5 instead of a calculator?
- you added 5 to a number and another 5 and another 5..?
- you tried subtracting fives — even beyond 0?

Aims

- thinking about what each digit in a two-digit number represents
- practising mental addition
- exploring number patterns
- predicting

Assessment points

Can children:
— mentally add 5 to any two-digit number?
— generalise about what kind of numbers will have both digits change when 5 is added to them?

Mathematical background information

Children will keep cards whose numbers end with 5, 6, 7, 8, 9 and return those whose numbers end with 0, 1, 2, 3, 4.

Organisation

When children pick the top card from a shuffled pack, it is a matter of chance whether or not both digits change. When the children become familiar with the activity get them to choose cards from a pack that has been spread out face up. This will encourage them to think carefully about which numbers 'work' and why they do.

Bubble 1

Encourage children to look at the cards thay are keeping and to see what they have in common — 'They all have high second digits', or 'There aren't any numbers ending in 3 or 4 or other low numbers'.

Bubble 2

It is important that children make predictions in this activity and don't just follow a mechanical routine.

Bubble 3

Some children may be able to work out that over time they will keep just as many cards as they return to the pack.

What if ...

Children who need to focus more closely on when and how the tens digit changes could try adding one instead of five each time.

If children use an abacus to add 5, it is very clear when both digits change, as a bead has to be added to the tens column.

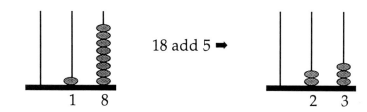

Where Is It?

Number (levels 2&3)
also
Using and applying mathematics

Ask the children to...

cover each number on the number square with a cube. Then each child takes a turn at picking a number card and trying to find and uncover that number on the board. When they have uncovered a number, they remove the cube.

The children may need...

Unifix 100-square grid
100-square
linking cubes
number cards 1-100
25-square and cards 1-25
squared paper

Useful questions

> What number have you got on your card? Roughly where will that number be?

> What number have you uncovered? Is that the right one?

> How did you find the number?

What if...

- you replaced the cubes each time?
- you used a different number grid — say 1-25 or 100-200?
- you used a number grid where the numbers were written in columns, or up and down, or in a spiral?
- you used an oblong number grid? Or some other shape?
- you used a blank grid and wrote in the number each time?
- you had a number grid each?

Aims

- thinking about the order of numbers
- getting to know the number system
- looking at number patterns
- predicting

Assessment points

Can children:
— read the number on their card?
— find the appropriate row for a number on a 100-square?
— find the appropriate column for a number on a 100-square?
— find the right place for a number on a 100-square?
— explain why a number belongs where it does?

Organisation

This activity can be used at a very simple level with a number line 0-10 or a number square 1-25. With young children you might choose to leave the numbers uncovered and let the activity become a simple matching exercise — children could cover up the number when they have found it on the grid.

With a large number grid (such as 1-100) this activity can take quite some time — especially the covering up of the number square with cubes. However it is a very useful diagnostic activity, especially if children are asked to explain how they found the number they were looking for.

Some cubes have holes in them. Children should place these on their sides, so they can't see through to the numbers underneath.

Bubble 1

It is worth checking that children can read the number on their card.

Bubble 2

Children will need to compare the number on their card with the one they have uncovered. If they have uncovered the wrong number, see if they can use the information they have gained to help them find the right place.

Bubble 3

Asking children how they found a number will give them the opportunity to explain all sorts of things they know about number patterns and the number system

What if . . .

This is a very versatile activity which can be adapted in all sorts of ways. Children can share a grid or have one each. They can use:
— grids with numbers written from bottom to top or in spirals
— grids showing decimal numbers
— grids showing negative numbers (for example, −50 to +50)
— grids with some numbers missing
— number lines instead of grids

One teacher used a large 1-30 grid, laminated with plastic. The numbers were covered up with Post-its and the children replaced these with the number cards they had picked at random from the pack.

Times Ten

Number (levels 2-4)
also
Using and applying mathematics

Ask the children to...

work in pairs. One child in each pair picks number cards at random from a pack of number cards, and the other child multiplies each number by 10. They should record their answers.

The children may need...

number cards (with a mixture of single-digit and two- and three-digit numbers)
calculators
number lines
cubes

Useful questions

Can you see any patterns?
Can you organise your recording to show those patterns?

Can you predict what you will get when you multiply that number by 10?

Can you read the numbers you have written?

What if...

- you displayed the original number, and the result, using base ten blocks or an abacus?

- you multiplied a number by 10 and then kept on multiplying the answer by 10?

- you divided numbers by 10, 100 or 1000?

- you multiplied the numbers by 20, 200 or 2000?

- you multiplied by 11, 111 or 1111?

- you multiplied by 0.1, 0.01 or 0.001?

Aims

- understanding the effect of multiplying whole numbers by 10 and 100
- exploring number patterns
- predicting

Assessment points

Can children:
- predict the result of multiplying any single-digit number by 10? By 100?
- predict the result of multiplying any two-digit number by 10? By 100?
- predict the result of multiplying any three-digit number by 10? By 100?

Organisation

Children could use a calculator and experiment with the constant function. However, many children will prefer to work it out in their heads.

Calculators are very valuable in this kind of work, but they alone cannot demonstrate how much larger 250 is than 25, whereas materials which model the size of a number can do this. So children will need to use a range of mathematical tools. Children could represent their numbers on an abacus. This shows clearly that a single-digit number, say 7, uses the same number of beads as 70, but in different positions. Base ten blocks and number lines could also be used.

Bubble 1

Children may get carried away with the activity at first and lose sight of the need to record. This is fine, as long as they are encouraged to make some records, and look at the patterns, at a later time.

Bubble 2

It is important that, as children become more familiar with this activity, they try to predict what numbers they will get.

Bubble 3

Children should be encouraged to share their understanding of what is going on with another pair. Putting what they see into words will help them clarify their ideas, and they may pick up new ways of seeing things. Sharing recording methods is also a good idea for the same reason.

You might ask them to collate their findings and put them on a larger chart to go on the wall.

What if ...

Starting with any number and continuing to multiply by 10 demonstrates clearly the way that 'noughts just keep adding to the right', (as one child put it).

Skittles

Number (levels 2-4)
also
Using and applying mathematics

Ask the children to...

work in pairs. Each child enters a three-digit (or higher) number in their calculator; they swap calculators and read out the number they have been given. They then have to replace the digits in the display, one by one, with 0. In each move they can use these buttons once: [−] [=] , and any one digit, and [0] as often as they need.

[1375]
↓
[1305]

The children may need...
calculators

Useful questions

In what order did you remove the digits?
How many subtractions did you do to remove each digit?

Could you reduce that same number to 0 another way?
A quicker way?

Can you record what you did?

What if...

- you removed one digit and your friend tried to put it back?
- you made this activity into a game?

- you invented your own rules?
- you used dice or a spinner to choose the starting number for you?

- you modelled what you are doing, on an abacus or number line?

- you entered a decimal fraction such as 23.45?
- you entered a negative number such as −2345?

Aims

- thinking about the exact value of each digit in a number
- working with large numbers
- planning their own work

Assessment points

Can children:
— read out a three- or four-digit number correctly?
— read out a higher number correctly?
— change a tens-digit to 0 in one move?
— change other digits to 0 in one move?

Mathematical background information

This is a very useful activity for assessing children's understanding of place value. Removing the digits can be done by more or less random subtractions, but if they are looking for an efficient way to do it then they need to use the structure of place value and remove one digit at a time.

```
367  - 7   = 360
360  - 300 = 60
60   - 60  = 0
```

Organisation

This activity deserves lots of discussion, so it is important to organise the session so that you are there to talk with children.

Some children might need to start with a two-digit number before going on to larger ones. If they still can't do it, suggest they remove ten at a time and see what happens.

If children can do this activity easily, they probably don't need to do it again at this level (try them on decimal or negative numbers). It is the children who get it a bit wrong who will benefit, through talking with you and each other, and through experimenting until they can see what they need to do.

Bubble 1

It doesn't matter in what order children remove the digits. However it is worth encouraging them to try to remove each digit with just one subtraction.

Bubble 2

Children may not realise at first that it does not matter which numeral they start with. For example, with the number 187 they can start by removing the 100 or the 80 or the 7.

Bubble 3

Recording their work can sometimes help children see not only that their methods are a bit cumbersome but also how to simplify them — especially if they share their records with each other.

What if...

Doing this activity with decimal fractions requires children to think about decimals, and underlines the fact that as far as place value is concerned these numbers 'work' in just the same way as whole numbers.

Working with negative numbers will, of course, mean adding numbers rather than subtracting. It might help children to start with two-digit negative numbers and model their 'moves' on a negative number line.

How Many Dots?

Number (levels 3-5)
also
Using and applying mathematics

Ask the children to...

estimate, then work out, the number of dots on one of the sheets. (There are two sheets in the *Photocopiables* section offering different levels of difficulty.)

The children may need...

How Many Dots? sheets
calculators

Useful questions

> Roughly how many dots do you think there are?

> How can you work it out?
> Might a calculator help you?

> How many sheets of dots like this would you need to make a thousand?
> A million?

What if...

- you made a sheet of dots like this on the computer for your friends to count?
- you counted the number of bricks in the school / hairs on your head / words in the telephone directory?
- you looked for other amazing things to count?
- you made a scrapbook about large numbers?

Aims

- developing a feel for large numbers
- estimating large numbers
- using addition
- thinking about the effects of multiplication and division
- thinking about strategies for counting large arrays

Assessment points

Can children:
— make a reasonable estimate of the number of dots on each sheet?
— find a way of calculating the number of dots?
— carry out their method successfully?

Mathematical background information

On one sheet there are 19 rows of 15 dots — 285. On the other there are 60 rows of 40 dots — 2,400 altogether. You can choose the sheet you want children to tackle depending on the appropriate level of difficulty.

Bubble 1

Encourage children to estimate the number of dots and write down their estimate. Children do not often have opportunities to see and work with such large numbers, so experiences like this are important to help them develop a feel for large numbers.

Bubble 2

Let children start counting each dot, if that is what they want to do. After a while they are likely to get lost and then is the time to help them think about other strategies such as counting blocks of a hundred or counting the rows and columns.

Bubble 3

285 is not a factor of 1000, nor is 2,400 a factor of 1,000,000 — so the answers are not neat ones. Four sheets of 285 would give a bit over 1000 (1140 in fact); 417 sheet of 2,400 would give a million dots and 800 over.

What if . . .

There are all kinds of things that come in large quantities that children could count, or estimate — for instance, people in all the schools in town, centicubes that could fit in the classroom, pages in the library. Children who become interested in large numbers could be directed to books such as the *Guinness Book of Records* where they can find interesting and amazing statistics.

Quadraville

Number (levels 3-5)
also
Using and applying mathematics

Ask the children to...

imagine visiting Quadraville where people have four instead of ten digits on their feet and on their hands. They hear a class of children counting "one, two, three, person, person-one, person-two ...".
Can they continue the counting?

The children may need...

counters
squared paper
abacus
multibase materials

Useful questions

- What happens after person?
  After person-one?
  After person-three?

- Which of our numbers do Quadraville people use?
  Which numbers do they not say?

- How high can you count in Quadraville numbers?
  Can you write Quadraville numbers?

What if...

- you drew some Quadraville creatures?

- you made a Quadraville number line?

- you made a Quadraville number square?

- you made up some Quadraville sums and gave them to your friends to work out the answers?

- you counted in Octaville numbers (up to 8) or some other system?

Aims

- working with bases other than 10
- getting a perspective on how number bases work
- seeing that base ten is only adopted as a matter of convention

Assessment points

Can children:
— follow the pattern of Quadraville counting?
— write a sequence of Quadraville numbers?

Mathematical background information

The Quadraville number called 'person' is like our 'ten' in that it represents all the fingers on one person's hand — but numerically it is worth what we call 'four'.

Quadraville numbers go like this:

name	value	written
one	one	1
two	two	2
three	three	3
person	four	10
person-one	five	11
person-two	six	12
person-three	seven	13

The next number could be called two-person (although children may find another name for it) and would be written 20.

If children get as high as the Quadraville number 100, 'person' persons (sixteen in our number system) they will need to find a word for that number, such as 'group' or 'crowd'.

Organisation

Children often find counting in other bases easier than adults do — perhaps because all counting systems are new to them and less ingrained. You could get children to hold up four fingers and use these to count with. This shows the logic behind calling a set of 'four' fingers 'person'.

In discussion with children you could point out that we use bases other than ten if we weigh things in pounds and ounces, or measure in feet and inches.

Bubbles 1 and 2

Children might find it helpful to model their numbers with multibase material in base four. If none is available children can make their own from squared paper.

| one | two | three | person |

Bubble 3

You could make this into a circular counting game — for instance, whoever gets a 'four' number (person, two-person, and so on) stands up. The last to stand up is the loser.

What if...

If children do 'sums' in Quadraville numbers they will come across what appear to be contradictions, such as 3 + 1 = 10. You can discuss why, in Quadraville, this makes sense.

You could prepare addition and multiplication grids for children to fill in. These will help them to see number patterns. If children want to investigate base eleven or twelve they will need symbols for ten and eleven. They could also invent base fourteen games using a pack of cards (Jack is eleven, Queen is twelve and so on).

How Big is a Million?

Number (levels 3-5)
also
Using and applying mathematics

Ask the children to...
make a million.

The children may need...
graph paper
base ten blocks
unnumbered number lines
calculators

Useful questions

- Could you start by making, say, a hundred?

- What materials are you making a million from?
  How big is the 'one' that you are making a million of?

- How big do you think a thousand will be?
  And a million?

What if...

- you had chosen a bigger/smaller 'one'?

- you made something that was a millionth ($1/_{1000000}$) of something else?

- you made a poster showing a million dots?

- you put a million grains of sand or water in the water tray?

Aims

- getting a feel for how big a million is
- understanding the relationships between hundreds, thousands and millions
- developing strategies for calculating and for displaying information
- working with measures
- ideas of scale

Assessment points

Can children:
— find ways of making and counting a thousand?
— discuss strategies for making a million?
— estimate how big a thousand of a chosen object would be?
— estimate how big a million of a chosen object would be?

Organisation

It is important for children to have experience of visualising numbers — especially large numbers, which they are less likely to see modelled with apparatus in the classroom.

This is a very open-ended activity. Some children may need considerable time discussing how they might show a million, while others dive in straight away. Possible starting points include:

— making dots on paper
— using base ten blocks (children will almost certainly not have enough to make a million 'ones' and will have to find a way round this)
— making a 3D frame from balsa wood or card that is as large as a million 'ones'
— making a number line in tens, hundreds or thousands

Bubble 1

Making a hundred or thousand may be enough of a challenge for some children.

Bubble 2

Children need to realise that a million of a large object is going to take up a lot more space than a million of a smaller object!

Bubble 3

Children can record their estimates and compare them with their actual results.

What if ...

You can use the idea of a million to work with all kinds of measures: a million seconds, litres, square centimetres, degrees Centigrade ...

Possible contexts

— history (time lines showing a million years or a million days or hours)

Target 500

Number (levels 3-6)
also
Using and applying mathematics

Ask the children to...

get into pairs and play *Target 500* — the game-sheet is in the *Photocopiables* section.

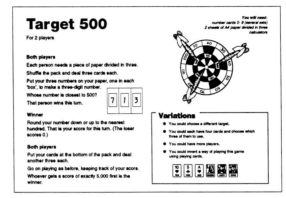

The children may need...

Target 500 game-sheet
calculators
number cards 0-9
(two sets at least)
number line 0-1000
(numbered in tens)

Useful questions

> What number have you made with your three cards?

> What is that digit worth? And that one?

> Whose number is closer to 500? How can you tell? Will you round that number up or down?

What if...

- you changed the target number?
- you changed the rules?

- three of you played together?
- you used four cards each time and had a higher target?

- you rounded to the nearest ten?

- you kept track of your score without using a calculator?

42

Aims

- getting a feel for place value
- understanding that the value of a digit depends on its position relative to other digits
- experience of rounding up and down

Assessment points

Can children:
— read out the three-digit number they have made?
— work out whose number is closer to 500?
— round their number up or down to the nearest hundred?

Organisation

You can teach this game to two children, with the help of the children's game-sheet, then those two can teach another two and so on. Then everyone in the class learns the game with just a small investment of your time.

Bubble 1

This question reminds children that what they have been doing is constructing a three-digit number.

Bubble 2

This question encourages children to put into words what they may only half understand — that the value of a digit depends on its position.

Bubble 3

Children can use calculators to find out whose number is closer to the target, but they may prefer to use a number line where the relative distances are easier to see.

What if ...

Children enjoy inventing their own rules for this game. For instance a group of children who played this game could not bear the vagueness of rounding up and down to find their scores at the end, but insisted on keeping a running total of the exact amount.

How Long is a Million?

Number (levels 4-6)
also
Using and applying mathematics

Ask the children to...

estimate how long it would take to count to one million, then work it out.

The children may need...

clocks and watches
stopwatch
calculators

Useful questions

- Do you intend to count up to a million? Have you got enough time?

- Does each number take the same amount of time to say? What about 'one' and '2,369'?

- How long would counting to 1000 take you? How does that knowledge help you?

What if...

- you counted to just 1000 or 10,000?

- you worked out how long it would take you to count to a billion?

- you estimated what else you could do in that time?

- you made a number line to a million? (Would you show every number?)

44

Aims

- getting a feel for how big a million is
- understanding the relationship between tens, hundreds, thousands and millions
- practice with calculating
- working with measures
- developing calculation strategies

Assessment points

Can children:
— develop sensible strategies for making an estimate of the length of time it would take to count to a thousand?
— develop sensible strategies for making an estimate of the length of time it would take to count to a million?
— calculate accurately with large numbers?

Organisation

Children may need reminding what the number 'a million' looks like on paper — 1,000,000 — and that there are 1000 thousands in a million.

Bubble 1

Encourage children to estimate how long the counting would take, and begin to test out their estimate. They will not be able to complete their count, so will need to do a calculation instead!

Bubble 2

Saying 'two thousand, three hundred and sixty-nine' takes considerably longer than saying 'one'. This means that children who want an accurate answer will have to do a more complex calculation than just multiplying up the length of time it takes to count to, say, 100. Of course *how* accurate they need to be is a matter for them — and you — to decide.

Bubble 3

Some children will be able to work out roughly how long it would take them to count to 1000 and want to stop there. Other children will be able to use that as a staging post on the way to the million problem.

What if . . .

Children could explore other answers to 'how long is a million?' — investigating where a million paces would take them, how far a million miles is, how the world has changed in the last million years . . .

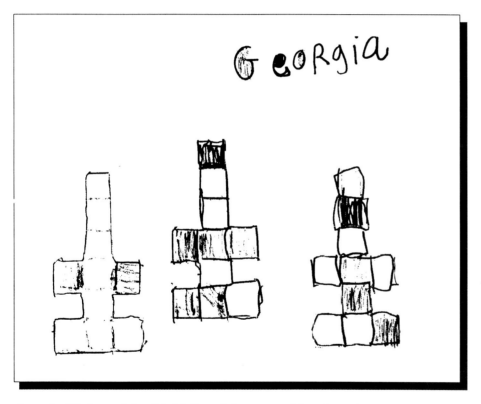

Georgia did the activity 'Cubist', and drew round her three figures.

$1563 \div 10 = 156.3$
$1563 \div 10 = 15.63$
$1563 \div 10 = 1.563$
0.1563
0.01563
0.01563
0.001563
0.0001563
0.00001563

Every time we divide it by 10 the dot moves up and when it gets to the end a nought comes up

Ben worked on an extension of 'Times Ten', repeatedly dividing a number by 10 to see what happened.

PHOTOCOPIABLES

Vegeburgers

For 2 players

You will need:
dice numbered 1, 1, 1, 2, 2, 2
counters (to use as burgers)
matchboxes (to use as boxes)
toy lorries (to load the boxes onto)

Take turns to toss the dice and say the number. Take that many burgers.

When you have collected 4 burgers, put them in a box. Only 4 burgers can go in a box.

When you have collected 4 boxes of burgers, put them on a lorry and drive them away.

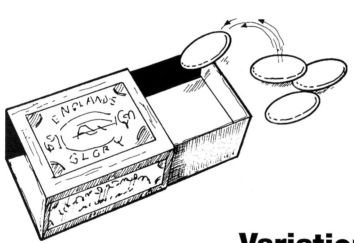

Variations

- You could put 5, 6 or 10 burgers in each box
- You could use a different dice
- When you have loaded the van up you could drive it off and unload it

© BEAM 1995

Swaps

You will need:
cards 0-30
0-30 or 0-100 number line

For 2 players

Deal three number cards each. Both of you, put your three numbers in order — like they are on the number line.

Now swap your middle card with your partner.

Look at your three cards now. Are they still in order?

If they are, write down the middle number. That is your score.

If not, you score 0 for that round.

Now deal another three cards and try again.

Keep doing this, adding your score each time, until one of you reaches 100 or more. That person wins.

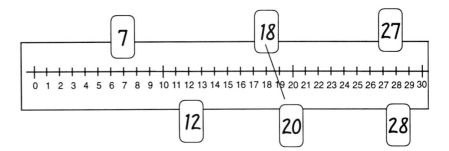

Variations

- You could play without a number line
- You could swap your high cards or your low cards
- You could use cards 0-50 or 0-100
- You could have five cards each, and swap middle cards with your friend

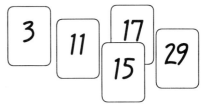

© BEAM 1995

Target 500

For 2 players

You will need:
number cards 0- 9 (several sets)
2 sheets of A4 paper divided in three
calculators

Both players

Each person needs a piece of paper divided in three.

Shuffle the pack and deal three cards each.

Put your three numbers on your paper, one in each 'box', to make a three-digit number.

Whose number is closest to 500?

That person wins this turn.

| 7 | 1 | 3 |

Winner

Round your number down or up to the nearest hundred. That is your score for this turn. (The loser scores 0.)

Both players

Put your cards at the bottom of the pack and deal another three each.

Go on playing as before, keeping track of your score.

Whoever gets a score of exactly 5,000 first is the winner.

Variations

- You could choose a different target.
- You could each have four cards and choose which three of them to use.
- You could have more players.
- You could invent a way of playing this game using playing cards.

© BEAM 1995

1	2	3	4	5	6	7	8	9	10
11	12	13	14	15	16	17	18	19	20
21	22	23	24	25	26	27	28	29	30
31	32	33	34	35	36	37	38	39	40
41	42	43	44	45	46	47	48	49	50
51	52	53	54	55	56	57	58	59	60
61	62	63	64	65	66	67	68	69	70
71	72	73	74	75	76	77	78	79	80
81	82	83	84	85	86	87	88	89	90
91	92	93	94	95	96	97	98	99	100

© BEAM 1995

1	2	3	4	5
6	7	8	9	10
11	12	13	14	15
16	17	18	19	20
21	22	23	24	25

© BEAM 1995

How many dots?

© BEAM 1995

How many dots?

© BEAM 1995

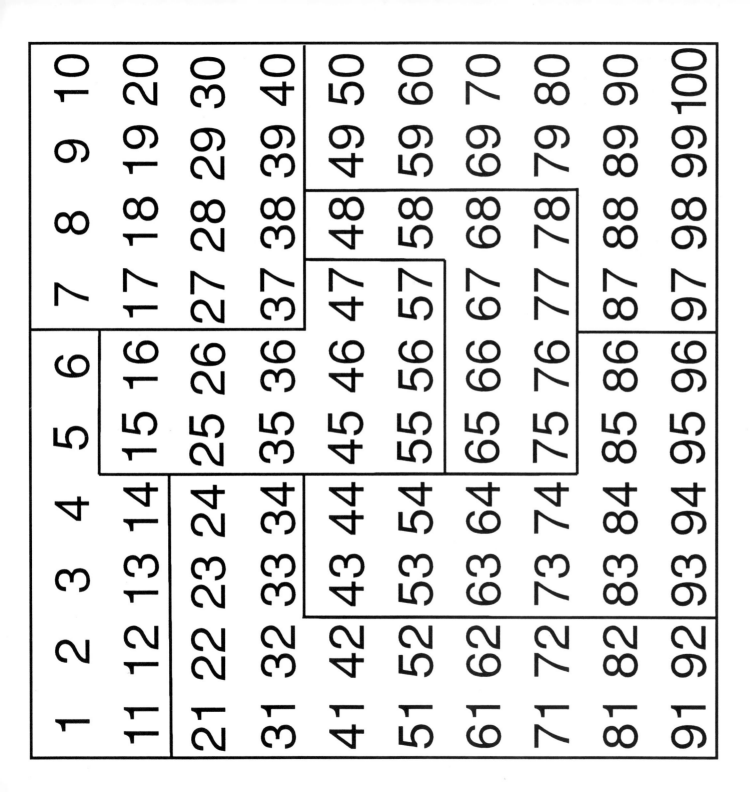

International Number Square Jigsaw

Cut out pieces along the thick lines.

© BEAM 1995

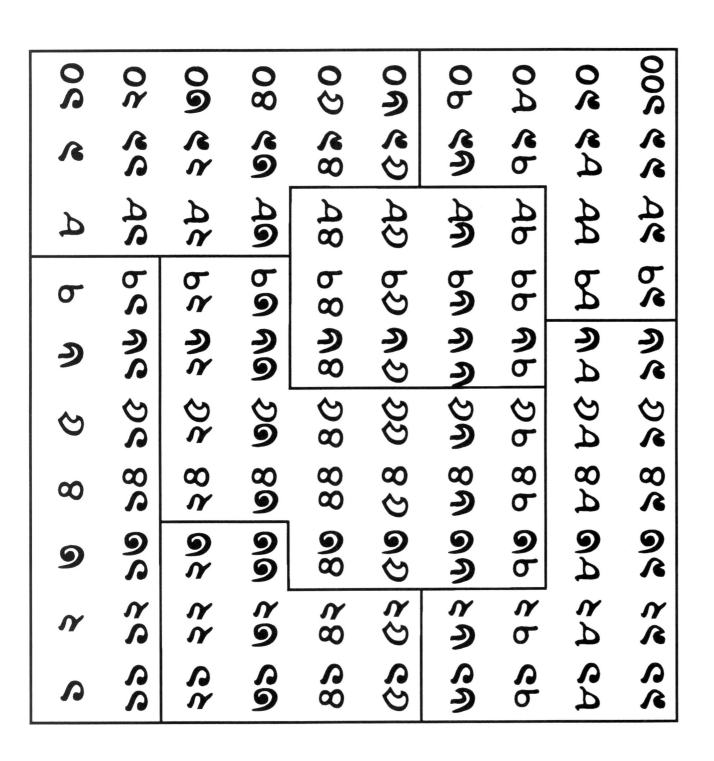

Bengali Number Square Jigsaw

Cut out pieces along the thick lines.

The Bengali numbers follow the same system as that used internationally and read left to right.

© BEAM 1995

Place value mat

Place value mat

Times Ten

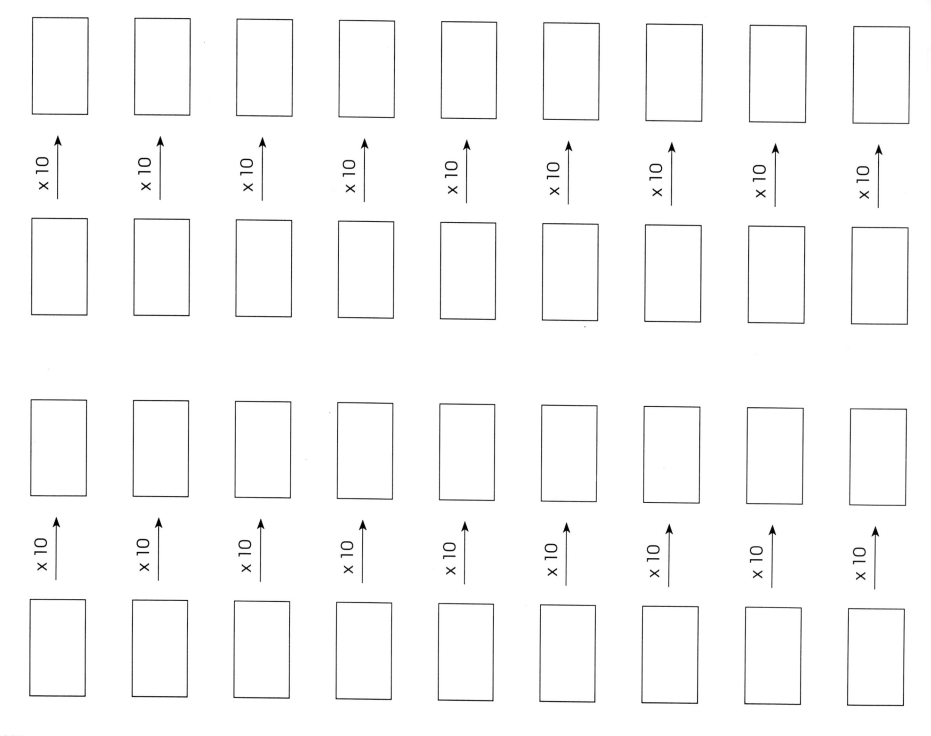

Sampling sheet

Name of child ....

Date	Name of activity and source	Social context and personal qualities	Number, Algebra, Shape & Space, Data-handling	Using and Applying Mathematics		
				Problem solving	Developing mathematical language	Developing mathematical reasoning

© BEAM 1995

Name	Activity
Date	

What I did

I used
- apparatus
- game
- writing
- computer
- calculator
- my head
- anything else

What maths I learnt

What I could do next

How I liked it

© BEAM 1995

RESOURCES

EQUIPMENT

The following is a list of equipment that will be useful (sometimes essential) to children doing the activities in this pack.

base ten blocks (and blocks in other bases)
bead abacus
calculators
clocks and watches
coins
computers
counters
cubes (including linking cubes such as Multilink and Unifix)
dice (blank)
graph paper
matchboxes
number cards
— 0-10
— 0-100
— spare blank cards

number lines
— unnumbered
— 0-30
— 0-50
— 0-100
— 0-1000
spinners
squared paper (1cm, 2cm and 5cm)
straws and rubber bands
toy lorries or other vehicles

and lead pencils, glue, card, paper, rulers, scissors, string, sticky tape and felt-tipped pens

RESOURCES

A Feel for Number
BEAM/King's College London/Tower Hamlets
ISBN 1 874099 32 4
This book contains activities which can be used to provide a number recovery programme for children in the middle and upper primary school who are experiencing difficulties. It can also be used with younger children. The book contains activities on number patterns and sequences, place value, and number operations. Each activity comes with variations and extensions for children who need plenty of practice. The book includes 30 pages of photocopiable materials — number squares, number lines and cards, worksheets and templates for games and activities.

Starting from Your Head: Mental Number
by David Fielker
BEAM   ISBN 1 874099 17 0
Visualisation and other forms of imagination are important skills in mathematical thinking, yet are often ignored in conventional teaching schemes. This book provides stimulating activities for you to offer children. The activities encourage children to analyse the processes they use, and challenge them to try out new ways of looking at numbers.

Starting from Scratch: Number
by Anna Lewis
BEAM   ISBN 1 874099 14 6
This book is for those teaching number at Key Stage 1. The activities appeal to children and lay the foundations for a sure understanding of number in later years.

Starting from Equipment: Number Lines
by Sue Gifford
BEAM   ISBN 1 874099 12 X
Number lines offer an important model of the number system, complementing the sets model that children meet more often. *Starting from Number Lines* contains dozens of interesting and valuable activities which use number lines to help children understand the relationships between numbers.

Exploring Decimals
BEAM   ISBN 1 874099 35 9
This is another of BEAM's activity books, like *Exploring Place Value*, and it contains 17 major activities on decimal numbers — decimal number notation, calculating with decimal numbers and so on. The activities take further some of the ideas introduced in this book, exploring the different values that digits have in different positions, including ones to the right of the decimal point. As well as the main activities there are photocopiable sheets of games, activities and record sheets.

Count Me In
AMS Educational   ISBN 0 7466 1179 X
This pack contains 23 number games for children at Key Stages 1 and 2. Each game is explained on a children's game-card, using clear simple language and cartoon illustrations — so the cards can be given directly to children. The games all use a set of 0-100 number cards, provided in the pack. A substantial teacher's book offers detailed suggestions on getting the most out of each game.

Working with Number Lines
by Helen Collison, Fran Mosley, Frances Purcell and Carole Skinner
AMS Educational   ISBN 0 7466 2599 5
This is a substantial book which tells you everything you need to know about using number lines in the classroom. It suggests dozens of activities to do with children who are learning about the place value number system, exploring how to jump in tens and hundreds, and generally becoming familiar with how numbers work.

Numbers in Place
AMS Educational
Unit 1   ISBN   0 7466 2121 3
Unit 2   ISBN   0 7466 2125 6
This consists of two packs each containing a range of resources for teaching about number and place value to children who are familiar with numbers up to 100 and are ready to go further. The materials include teacher's books offering practical help with classroom organisation as well as background information, and activity cards and books for children.

Numbers in Place Mats
AMS Educational   ISBN 1 0 7466 2145 0
These are bright washable plastic mats, each divided into three sections to enable children to represent whole and decimal numbers using materials such as base ten bocks or bundles of straws and number tablets.

Let's Start Decimals
Pictorial Charts Educational Trust, 27 Kirchen Road, London W13 0UD
Tel 0181-567 9206
Let's Start Decimals is a large chart based on a picture of a school in the process of being built. The picture shows various situations in which decimal numbers are used — someone turning a radio dial, two people poring over a scale plan of the site, and so on. Round the edge are various activities for children to engage with. The teacher's notes suggest ways of introducing these activities to children. Suitable for Key Stage 2.

Let's Do Decimals
Pictorial Charts Educational Trust, 27 Kirchen Road, London W13 0UD
Tel 0181-567 9206
Let's Do Decimals consists of six small full-colour posters, containing intriguing and challenging activities to do with decimals. The teacher's notes suggest ways of introducing these activities to children. Suitable for Key Stage 2.

Talking Points in Mathematics
by Anita Straker
Cambridge University Press   ISBN 0 521 44758 5
This important book contains hundreds of mathematical activities which children can do and discuss — the emphasis is very much on talking, debating, searching for understanding through sharing ideas with others.

The Million Poster
Tarquin Publications, Stradbroke, Diss, Norfolk IP21 5JP
Tel 01379 384218   Fax 01379 384289
This poster shows one million dots in a strongly structured way and also poses some questions to stimulate children's thinking.

Primary Mathematics Today
by Elizabeth Williams and Hilary Shuard
Longman   ISBN 0 582 36004 8
This book is an essential part of any primary and middle school library. It provides the non-specialist teacher with information on almost every aspect of primary mathematics, including place value. The book offers an explanation of the mathematics, and makes suggestions about teaching each topic to children.

Slimwam 2
Association of Teachers of Mathematics, 7 Shaftesbury Street, Derby DE23 8YB
Tel 01332 346599   Fax 01332 204357
This is a collection of six computer programs for children. Two of them, Monty and Counter, are useful as extensions to activities in this pack. Slimwam 2 is available for BBC, Archimedes and Nimbus.

Mathematics in Primary Schools
Part 1: Children and Mathematics
by Sheila Ebbutt, Anita Straker and Fran Mosley
HarperCollins   ISBN 0 7466 0046 1
Part 2: Making it Happen
by Sheila Ebbutt and Anita Straker
AMS Educational   ISBN 0 7466 0047 X
BEAM Starters
by the BEAM writing team
HarperCollins   ISBN 0 7466 0045 3
The three books in this series were written by ILEA teachers and inspectors as a resource for schools. *Part 1* is for all teachers. It provides an overview of mathematics and gives detailed help with integrating technology into the curriculum and adopting an investigative approach to mathematics. *Part 2* is for those with responsibility for mathematics in school, and advisors. It discusses methods of designing and putting into practice a school policy on mathematics, and debates topics such as provision of equal opportunities and home-school links. *BEAM Starters* provides a set of starting points for mathematical activity.